The English Phrasal Verbs Workbook

Dimitri Tsekouras
Wendy Ball
Dimitra Zacharopoulou

Edward Arnold
A division of Hodder & Stoughton
LONDON MELBOURNE AUCKLAND

© 1990 Tsekouras, Ball, Zacharopoulou

First published in Great Britain 1990

Illustrated by Sophie Grillet

British Library Cataloguing in Publication Data

British Library Cataloguing in Publication data
Tsekouras, Dimitri
   The English phrasal verbs workbook.
   1. English language. Phrasal verbs.
   I. Title II. Ball, Wendy III. Zacharopolou, Dimitra
   425

   ISBN 0-340-50032-8

Typeset in English Times and Gill by Brian Smith Partnership, Bristol

Printed and bound in Great Britain for Edward Arnold,
the educational, academic and publishing division of Hodder and
Stoughton Limited, Mill Road, Dunton Green, Sevenoaks,
Kent TN13 2YA by St Edmundsbury Press, St Edmundsbury.

CONTENTS

Introduction

Phrasal verbs are verbs that combine with an adverbial and/or prepositional particle to create a single verbal unit. Phrasal verbs are apparently simple in concept, but because of their idiomatic use and compound nature, they can cause considerable problems for the non-native speaker. The English Phrasal Verbs Workbook offers the opportunity to practise using phrasal verbs in a structured way so that the student can learn through doing the exercises and consulting the Key. It is intended for students who have reached an intermediate or advanced level of English and it can be used in class or for private study.

The English Phrasal Verbs Workbook offers practice material for all the verb bases described in the successful and highly popular English Phrasal Verbs in . . . series of reference books. The Workbook follows the same alphabetical method of organization and consists of five sections, each divided into two parts. Part One focuses on the grammatical elements of phrasal verb usage, and Part Two focuses on semantic points. The exercises in each section have been designed to take the student from first recognition to language production in six progressive stages. In this way the student will be able to learn as well as to build on previous knowledge.

Section One: Part One

EXERCISE ONE

Read the following sentences. Think carefully about the word order and whether the verb is separable or inseparable. Some of the sentences are correct and some are incorrect. Put a tick (√) in the box by the sentences that are correct. Put a cross (×) in the box by the sentences that are incorrect. Check your answers with the Key.

1 The managers did not agree with the workers. ☐

2 He backed his agreement out of because he was afraid. ☐

3 The reporter backed his story up with some hard facts. ☐

4 Some of the terrorists wanted to blow them up. ☐

5 Burglars broke the offices into and stole some important papers. ☐

6 The journalist said that he would call the man back immediately. ☐

7 To be a successful journalist calls for a certain amount of courage. ☐

8 The police car was more powerful and caught up with quickly the stolen car. ☐

EXERCISE TWO

The following paragraph is about a British Labour Party Conference. In the final debate, did some people disagree with the leader of the Labour Party? Read the paragraph and check your answer with the Key.

Last night saw the final debate in this year's Labour Party Conference. As expected, there were repeated calls to break away from the old traditions and to bring in all the reforms necessary to change the party's image. The party leader made his position clear by stating that he had no intention of bringing back the dogma of the past and called on unionists to support this new campaign. He said that they were through with outdated loyalties and that they were ready to move into the twenty-first century. A few shouts from the back of the hall bore out the fact that the party was not as unified as the leader hoped. However, the conference broke up with the usual statements of solidarity.

When you have read the paragraph, underline all the phrasal verbs. Circle the nouns that are directly related to each phrasal verb and draw arrows from the nouns to the verb. Check your answers with the Key.

Examples: (He) carried out his (threat.)

(He) gave his word to call back the (agent.)

EXERCISE THREE

The sentences below are incomplete. Study the sentences and decide what *kind* of word is needed to complete each sentence: a verb, or a phrasal verb particle, or a noun, or an adjective, or an adverb. Write down the kind of word needed in the box at the end of each sentence. Check your answers with the Key.

Example: In spite of the noise, they carried (quietly/soft/on) talking.

| particle |

1 The priest was (singing/about/quiet) to say, 'I pronounce you man and wife,' when someone ran in shouting, 'Stop! Stop!'

2 That girl (in/rich/is) out to get herself a wealthy husband.

3 He tried to (be/carefully/often) out every time his mother-in-law came to visit.

4 His wife was sure that he was up (wicked/the mistress/to) something as he kept coming home late.

5 His parents had to know sooner or later that he wanted to become a dancer, so he brought (the subject/quickly/explaining) up when he was home for the weekend.

6 A dancer fainted from the heat on stage but they brought her (carefully/comfortable/round) by carrying her outside into the fresh air.

7 To ensure success, some of the best dancers in the world were brought under (studied/the direction/in) of a brilliant Russian choreographer.

8 The date of the final performance was (the day/conveniently/over) brought forward to coincide with a visit from the Australian Prime Minister.

2

9 The praise from his instructor brought out (his talent/often/after).

10 The director brought in a brilliant but (man/beautifully/ unknown) dancer to dance the lead.

When you have decided what kind of word is needed to complete each sentence, look at the list of words given in brackets. Choose the correct word and complete the sentence.

Example: In spite of the noise, they carried (quietly/soft/on) talking.

EXERCISE FOUR

Look at the sentences below. Which sentences would be grammatically correct without the phrase in brackets and which would be incorrect without the phrase in brackets? Remember that some phrasal verbs are transitive − they must be followed by an object. For your answers underline the phrases that can be omitted and then check the Key.

Example: The dog smelt the scent and was off (like a shot).

The dog was old and could not catch up with (the fox).

1 She was so upset that she blew up (at the policeman).

2 The report was backed up (with very strong evidence).

3 When they interviewed her on the television she broke down (in tears).

4 The young man offered a bribe because he was after (quick and easy success).

5 The house had been broken into (seventeen times).

6 On Saturday he was in (washing the floor).

7 The headmistress bore down on (the girls smoking in the corner).

8 He said that he would be along (with a friend).

9 The farmer would not agree to (the price being offered).

10 As the growling dog approached, she backed away (against the wall).

11 The teacher told all the class to carry on (with their work whilst he was out of the classroom).

12 All over the world people are calling for (greater democracy).

13 The Prime Minister bore up (under critical questioning).

14 Greed for money brings out (the worst in people).

15 All evening he had to bear with (her boring conversation).

Where possible in the following sentences, change the noun phrases in brackets to pronouns *without changing the order of the words*. Remember that the particle of a separable phrasal verb must follow an object pronoun.

Example: (The athlete) carried off (the first prize).

He carried off the first prize NOT *He carried off it.*

16 (The chief) brought (his wife) through (her terrible illness).

17 (The leader) broke up (the bread) and gave each of (his followers) a piece.

18 (The shop steward) called out (the workers).

19 (The boilerman) cleared (the ashes) away before lighting (the fire).

How could you add an adverb to the following sentences? Which of the numbered places would be most suitable for the adverb in brackets?

20 ^{1}He^{2}backed^{3}up^{4}the decision.^{5} (firmly)

21 ^{1}He^{2}called^{3}back^{4}to confirm his booking.^{5} (immediately)

22 ^{1}It^{2}bears^{3}upon^{4}the matter to hand.^{5} (directly)

EXERCISE FIVE

Make sentences using the words given below. (The words may not be in the correct order.) Again, think carefully about the position of the object pronoun and check your answers with the Key.

Example: (a) The boy / the balloon / blew / up

The boy blew the balloon up. or **The boy blew up the balloon.**

     (b) He / it / blew / up

     He blew it up.

1 (a) The burglar / the house / broke / into
  (b) He / it / broke / into

2 (a) The young woman / the colt / broke / in
  (b) She / it / broke / in

3 (a) The draught / the candles / blew / out
  (b) It / them / blew / out

4 (a) The young analyst / the meeting / blew / into
  (b) He / it / blew / into

5 (a) Conservative people / capital punishment / would bring / back
  (b) They / it / would bring / back

6 (a) The photograph / memories / brought / back
  (b) It / them / brought / back

Rewrite the following sentences in the passive. Do not include the agents in your sentences.

Example: The bulldozer cleared the debris away.

The debris was cleared away.

7 The mechanic brought the car back.

8 They called him back for interview.

9 The members agreed upon the decision last Wednesday.

10 The landlord cleared the flat out for the incoming tenants.

11 They eventually caught him out with some clever questioning.

EXERCISE SIX

Using each of the sentences below to help you, make new sentences by replacing the phrases in brackets with grammatically correct phrases of your own. Check the Key for model answers.

Example: (Happiness) calls for (a certain amount of good fortune).

A successful business calls for good management.

1 The committee members all agreed to (elect a new chairman).

2 The cottage backed onto (an old orchard full of ancient apple trees).

3 He was for (shooting the sick dog).

4 In his disillusionment he felt that he was through with (trusting women).

5 The footballer's moment of triumph was over as (the police moved in to arrest him).

6 He blew (the balloon) up and (gave it to the child).

7 The date of the meeting has been brought forward (so that I can go on holiday the week after).

8 With some expert manipulating he brought (the committee) round (to his viewpoint).

9 He called upon (his friends to support his claim).

10 He carried (his threat) out and (stopped their water supply).

11 (The new cell telephone) has caught on with the (wealthy young professionals).

12 The rash on his face and hands cleared up (after he stopped handling the chemical sprays).

Section One: Part Two

EXERCISE ONE

Read the following sentences. There is a short list of verbs accompanying each sentence. From the list, find the verb that is the closest in meaning to the underlined verb in the sentence. Circle your answer and then check the Key.

1 He <u>agreed with</u> current opinion and thought that more money should be spent on the environment.

> corresponded with
> approved of
> accepted
> combined with

2 The footballer <u>backed out of</u> the contract when he found out that he would have to live abroad.

> withdrew from
> disagreed with
> reversed
> derived

3 The bounty hunter <u>was after</u> the treasure.

> cherished
> wanted
> dug for
> came behind

4 The schedule for motorway repairs <u>is way behind</u> and this is adding to the traffic problems.

> is improved
> is delayed
> is inferior
> continues

5 Batman <u>is on</u> at the Odeon Cinema.

> is going to take place
> is visiting
> is arriving
> is showing

6 She asked him <u>to bear with</u> her nervousness of snakes as she had once been bitten.

> to understand
> to support
> to be patient with
> to relate to

7 The trouble soon <u>blew over</u> and everyone pretended that nothing had happened.

> subsided
> developed
> surfaced
> disappeared

8 He <u>broke away from</u> tradition and married an outsider.

> destroyed
> renounced
> refused
> gave up

6

9 The international talks broke down as there were no grounds for agreement.

were discontinued
were destroyed
collapsed
were reduced

10 The resignation of the senior minister brought about the collapse of the government.

approximated
purchased
produced
caused

11 Wetting the stones brings out their colour.

reveals
publishes
departs
accompanies

12 The people called for a right to vote.

cried for
campaigned for
demanded
fetched

13 Despite the warning sign, he carried on driving fast.

continued
behaved
managed
supported

14 The farmers caught on to this new development and began to increase their field size to take the new machines.

used
popularized
understood
drew level with

15 The fog cleared away to reveal the house, the fields and the sea beyond.

disappeared
removed
raised
clarified

EXERCISE TWO

The following paragraph is about the money market response to a speech by the Chancellor of the Exchequer. In the speech, did the Chancellor say that he was going to change his policies or did he say that he was going to continue his present policies? Read the paragraph and check your answer with the Key.

This morning the pound bore up in spite of decreasing confidence in the money markets, but it was definitely down after the Chancellor's speech this afternoon. Although some financial experts are saying that the Stock Exchange has blown the problem up out of all proportion, it is true to say that most people were not impressed with the Chancellor's statements. He stated that he was determined to carry through his previously stated policies in the belief that they were the best for Britain and that no amount of ineffectual, uninformed criticism would make him back down. By the end of his speech the Chancellor had failed to clear the doubts away completely but he was given the now usual standing ovation.

Answer the questions below by putting a tick (√) in the box for yes or the box for no.

	YES	NO
1 Did the pound remain strong this morning?	☐	☐
2 Did the pound remain strong this afternoon?	☐	☐
3 Have the financial experts made the problem larger?	☐	☐
4 Are the experts saying the Stock Exchange has made the problem larger?	☐	☐
5 Is the Chancellor going to carry through his belief?	☐	☐
6 Is the Chancellor saying that his policies will continue in action?	☐	☐
7 Does the Chancellor want to reverse his decision if there is criticism?	☐	☐
8 Is the Chancellor going to stand up to his critics?	☐	☐
9 Were some of the listeners doubtful after the Chancellor's speech?	☐	☐
10 Did the Chancellor completely fail to persuade his listeners?	☐	☐

EXERCISE THREE

Complete the following paragraph using words from the list below. There is one word for each gap and each word in the list can be used only once. Check your answers with the Key.

broken	~~backs~~	bringing	bearing	catch
up	on	onto	~~into~~	with	off

Burglars committed a daring crime last night in the seaside resort of Seaton. One of the High Street banks was _____ **into** and a marble statue of the bank's original owner was stolen. It is not known how the thieves gained entry to the bank, and it is certainly not known how they managed to escape with a 200kg lump of marble. The bank **backs** _____ a vacant plot of land and this probably made access easier. It is known that certain of the bank's employees were very angry at some changes that are planned for the bank and this may well have a _____ _____ the case. Doubtless the authorities will _____ _____ _____ the culprits, but the question that must be in everyone's mind is: 'Why go to the trouble of _____ _____ such a pointless and risky robbery?'

EXERCISE FOUR

There are some words missing from the sentences below. Use the missing words (putting the verbs into the infinitive) to complete the puzzle.

1 This is such an important point you ought to _____ it up at the next meeting.

2 The problem of whom should be ultimately responsible was never _____ up.

3 The leader _____ all for the execution of the murderer.

4 They couldn't make up their minds and no one was sure whether the engagement _____ off or on.

5 A scouting party _____ away from the main army.

6 When he realised that he was in the minority, he backed _____.

7 The facts gathered by the police officer were borne _____ by the eyewitness's account.

8 At the outbreak of war he was called _____.

9 He had to work overtime as he was _____ with his work.

10 The love and support offered by her family helped carry her _____ that difficult time.

11 Although Telly Savalas is _____ he has been in many American films.

12 There is no _____ in my mind that satellite television will catch on.

```
                    11          12
   1 ☐ ☐ ☐ ☐ ☐      6 ☐ ☐ ☐ ☐
   2 ☐ ☐ ☐ ☐ ☐      7 ☐ ☐ ☐
           3 ☐ ☐     8 ☐ ☐
           4 ☐ ☐     9 ☐ ☐ ☐ ☐ ☐ ☐
   5 ☐ ☐ ☐ ☐ ☐     10 ☐ ☐ ☐ ☐ ☐ ☐ ☐
```

EXERCISE FIVE

In the following text the writer is discussing an environmental issue. Read the paragraph and decide if the writer owns a car. Check your answer with the Key. Then read the text again and answer the questions below.

If only the government would agree upon some policy for transport that made some sense. Back in 1972 it was predicted that a total seizure of the road system in Britain could occur if the only solution to the increase in traffic was to pour more money into the system. As the government continues to carry out this policy a total seizure seems inevitable.

What other alternatives are there? It is not so long ago that everyone was down on the public transport system and for the independence that a private car can offer, but now public opinion is moving in a different direction. People are becoming more aware of the pressure of traffic as they see the roads are crowded, the towns and cities choked with cars, the noise and pollution only too apparent. Surprisingly, economic pressure may not change transport policies but environmental concern might. Concern for the environment has now become a political issue; the speed at which unleaded petrol has caught on bears this out. Because environmental conservation is politically important, conservationists might now have the power to change transport policies.

However, politics alone will not bring about any radical change in transport policy or in the degree of environmental damage caused by cars. The only real solution calls for everyone to give up their car. We have to break away from the control that this most desired machine has on our civilisation. The car controls the development of economies, it affects the design of our communities, it uses up a larger amount of finite natural resources than any other commodity, and the numbers of deaths it causes are way over those caused by war. Whatever one's personal opinion, it is becoming self-evident that if we all carry on driving our own car, our transport systems will seize up, and, on a global scale, the earth's atmosphere cannot bear up against limitless man-made pollution.

1 What is the writer's opinion of present government policy for transport?

2 What transport policy is the government continuing to put into practice?

3 A short time ago, was public opinion in favour of public or independent transport?

4 Are the public keen to buy unleaded petrol?

5 What does the popularity of unleaded petrol prove?

6 In the writer's opinion, will politics alone cause a radical change in transport policies?

7 What does the writer believe is the most effective way to halt the environmental damage being done by cars?

8 In the opinion of the writer we need to be freed. What do we need to be freed from?

9 If we all continue to drive our own car, what will happen and why?

EXERCISE SIX

Read the following informal conversation between a supervisor, Mr White, and a technician, Mr Blue.

Mr White: You're late.

Mr Blue: It's only 10 o'clock.

Mr White: Work starts at 9. You can't just come into work whenever you feel like it.

Mr Blue: It's only that getting up early doesn't agree with me.

Mr White: Look, I've had a report in from the boss. He says your work's off and your calculations are way out. I'd like to know what's going on.

Mr Blue: I've got a few personal problems, that's all. I'll catch up with my work by doing overtime.

Mr White: Not so fast, young man. These problems of yours aren't just going to blow over. You work with a team and this carry-on is making things difficult for everyone. Your attitude calls for a major change. Otherwise, my lad, you can clear out of here.

If Mr Blue had the same conversation with the managing director, Mr Power, it would be more formal. The phrasal verbs would probably be replaced by non-phrasal verbs. Complete the conversation below using more formal language, remembering that there are many ways of doing this. There is a model answer in the Key.

Mr Power: I see that you are rather late today.

Mr Blue: Yes, but I'm not very late.

Mr Power: I should like to point out that work begins at 9 o'clock. You can't just come into work whenever you feel like it.

Mr Blue: It's only that getting up early doesn't agree with me.

Mr Power: Look, I've written a report which says that your work . . .

Section Two: Part One

EXERCISE ONE

Read the following sentences. Think carefully about the word order and whether the verb is separable or inseparable. Some of the sentences are correct and some are incorrect. Put a tick (√) in the box by the sentences that are correct. Put a cross (×) in the box by the sentences that are incorrect. Check your answers with the Key.

1 The doctor cut the shoe away to look at the player's injured foot. ☐

2 The defending players cut the line of attack off to the goal. ☐

3 The football manager thought that the team could do another week of training with. ☐

4 The number of football spectators has fallen off because of the hooligans. ☐

5 The cricket club had a plan to improve the changing rooms but they have given up it because of the cost. ☐

6 They were giving away autographed team photographs as a publicity stunt. ☐

7 The bus drew in front of the stadium up and the players got out. ☐

8 The athlete carefully did the laces up on his training shoes. ☐

EXERCISE TWO

The following paragraph describes a golf tournament. How many players are mentioned in the text? Read the paragraph and check your answer with the Key.

Yesterday's golf tournament at St Andrews came up to expectations, giving all the players a chance to prove their worth under soggy conditions and buffeted by a merciless wind. Surprisingly, the champion, Brian Treadmill, fell behind after the ninth hole when he drove the ball into a bunker and took an extra three strokes to extricate himself. At the twelfth hole Terry Sanders went ahead by two strokes, which left him at three under par. By the fifteenth hole he was having difficulties with the wet and muddy course and he had to draw on all his experience to get out of some very awkward situations. At the end of a wet and exhausting day's play it was David Perkins who came across as the player with the most confidence and with the most likely chance of getting through to the final. When asked for his opinion on the bad conditions, he said, 'You've just got to do your best, keep your head and get on with the game.'

When you have read the paragraph, underline all the phrasal verbs. Circle the nouns that are directly related to each phrasal verb and draw arrows from the nouns to the verb. Check your answers with the Key.

Examples: He got through the course in spite of feeling exhausted.

He had to do with a number nine iron as he had forgotten his woods.

EXERCISE THREE

The sentences below are incomplete. Study the sentences and decide what *kind* of word is needed to complete each sentence: a verb, or a phrasal verb particle, or a noun, or an adjective, or an adverb. Write down the kind of word needed in the box at the end of each sentence. Check your answers with the Key.

Example: The salesman (on/came/right) across as a very honest man. | Verb |

1 It took him a long time to get (sadly/over/forgiving) his disappointment at not getting the job. | |

2 By asking for school leavers in the advertisement they were trying to get out of (paying/into/cleverly) larger salaries. | |

3 He was trying to get round (stolen/over/the tax laws) by investing in a business running at a loss. | |

4 They were getting along (good/very well/the work) with the data processing when there was a power failure. | |

5 The sales manager was trying to get (clear/the idea/over) across to the foreign client but he did not seem to realise that there was a language problem. | |

6 We're thinking of getting into the (modernise/newly/latest) technology next year. | |

13

7 The inspectors are (coming/visitor/punctual) round at midday.

8 From the sales figures for this year, I think we can confidently expect to come (the statistics/compete/up) to the same level as our competitors.

9 (Lied/Bad/The truth) came out and his resignation was called for.

10 After two years away, he came back from (America/round/adventurous) and joined the accounting department.

When you have decided what kind of word is needed to complete each sentence, look at the list of words given in brackets. Choose the correct word and complete the sentence.

Example: The salesman (on/came/right) across as a very honest man.

EXERCISE FOUR

Look at the sentences below. Which sentences would be grammatically correct without the phrase in brackets and which would be incorrect without the phrase in brackets? Remember that some phrasal verbs are transitive — they must be followed by an object. For your answers underline the phrases that can be omitted and then check the Key.

Example: His mother spoiled all her children. Whenever they demanded anything, she used to give in (and let them have what they wanted).

1 She had no idea when he was coming back (until she received his first letter).

2 At the fair, they were giving away (balloons to all the children).

3 The floods were so bad last night, they came up to (the 1955 flood levels).

4 She told the policeman to come in (and have a cup of tea).

5 When the visitors came to the factory, they asked the men to carry on (working).

6 Part of a film editor's job is to cut out (all the offensive shots).

7 The company stands to make a lot of money, if the deal comes off (next week).

8 His life fell apart (after his wife's death).

9 Mrs Jenkins has done for (Mr Jones for more than twelve years).

10 They came to a narrow path along the river. He fell back (to let her go first).

14

11 The tour bus drew up (outside the hotel).

12 By taking a short cut, he managed to catch up with (his friends).

13 She's rather elderly and finds it difficult to get about (the house to do the housework).

14 We're not close friends but we get along (well enough to go out together once a week).

Where possible in the following sentences, change the noun phrases in brackets to pronouns *without changing the order of the words.* Remember that the particle of a separable phrasal verb must follow an object pronoun.

Example: (The cook) cut up (the pie) into equal portions.

He cut up the pie into equal portions.NOT *He cut up it into equal portions.*

15 (The warrior) cut (his enemy's head) off with his sword.

16 (The police) managed to get back (the purse) that was stolen.

17 (The shop assistants) were giving away (samples) to promote the new product.

18 (The little boy) refused to give (the knife) back to (his father).

19 Although the doctors feared the worst, (the patient) came through (his fever).

How could you add an adverb to the following sentences? Which of the numbered places would be most suitable for the adverb in brackets?

20 ¹Nobody could²come³up⁴with⁵any ideas⁶ (immediately)

21 ¹Bluebeard²did³away⁴with⁵all of his wives⁶ (brutally)

22 ¹As he had no income,²he³fell⁴behind⁵with⁶his payments⁷ (inevitably)

23 ¹Whilst walking along with the group,²he³fell⁴behind⁵to look at the view⁶ (quietly)

EXERCISE FIVE

Make sentences using the words given below. (The words may not be in the correct order.) Again, think carefully about the position of the object pronoun and check your answers with the Key.

Example: (a) The prisoner / books / did / without

The prisoner did without books.

(b) He / them / did / without

He did without them.

1 (a) The new technology / costs / cuts/ down
  (b) It / them / cuts / down
2 (a) A well-tuned engine / fuel consumption / cuts / down / on
  (b) It / it / cuts / down / on
3 (a) The policeman / the address / got / down
  (b) He / it / got / down
4 (a) The man / his work / got / down / to
  (b) He / it / got / down / to
5 (a) The teacher / the exam papers / gave / out
  (b) He / them / gave / out

Make questions from the following words.

6 the quarrel / did / come / how / about /?
7 with / any / up / did / come / ideas / he /?
8 he / cut / was / off / why / from his inheritance /?
9 with / he / fall / who / did / in /?
10 will / away / get / it / with / he /?
11 some work / down / to / going / he / when / get / to / is /?

EXERCISE SIX

Using each of the sentences below to help you, make new sentences by replacing the phrases in brackets with grammatically correct phrases of your own. Check the Key for model answers.

Example: (The old lady) was done out of (a thousand pounds).

I was done out of my inheritance.

1 (The dealer) came by (the old coins) on his visit to Germany.
2 (My son) is coming on (at his new school).
3 (A look of horror) came over (the woman's face) as she realised (that she could have been killed).
4 (The farmers) cut back (the forest) to (make a clearing).
5 (The young man) felt that he was cut out for (a life of leisure).
6 (The young man) fell in with (a bad crowd) whilst he was (at college).
7 (The advertisement for face cream) got (the idea of softness) across by (using a picture of a child).
8 (The gorilla) couldn't get at (the bananas) and (it was becoming frustrated).
9 It was a long time before (the child) got over (the death of her pet bird).
10 It was six months before (the developers) got (the planning stage) over so that (the building could begin).

16

Section Two: Part Two

EXERCISE ONE

Match each of the expressions below to one of the following cartoons. Write the number of the expression next to the letter of the cartoon, e.g. (j)1. Check your answers with the Key.

1 Fall in.
2 I'm done for.
3 Get out!
4 Get up!
5 What a giveaway!
6 Give in.
7 Come in.
8 Come on!
9 Get on.
10 I won't give up!

EXERCISE TWO

The following text gives people advice on how to stop smoking. Where would you find this kind of text – in a scientific journal, in a government leaflet, in a school textbook, in a popular magazine? Read the text and check your answer with the Key.

Smoking is a hard habit to break, but an increasing number of people are giving up and many of them say they found it easier to stop than they thought it would be.

Although non-smoking lobbies are now coming down hard on smokers, most people who smoke are coming round to the idea that smoking is indeed bad for your health. Women smokers are particularly at risk, usually because of cervical cancer. Smoking kills 40,000 women in Britain each year. Pregnant smokers increase the risk of miscarriage and have babies of low birth weight. Children of smokers are more likely to get colds and chest infections.

Nine out of ten people who stop smoking do it on their own, but there are ways to make it easier. If you find it difficult to get through the day without a cigarette, the following points might help.

● Try to avoid situations where you usually smoke – get into a different daily routine.

● Don't cut out cigarettes completely, cut down gradually on the number you smoke each day until one day you will find that you can do without.

● Give yourself treats to reward yourself for not smoking.

Once you have stopped, try not to give in to temptation. It might help to talk to people experiencing the same problem. If you have a relapse, do not give up. Most people have to make a few attempts before they succeed in stopping altogether. For more information and advice, contact ASH (Action on Smoking and Health), 5–11 Mortimer Street, London.

Answer the questions below by putting a tick (√) in the box for yes or the box for no.

	YES	NO
1 In the first paragraph, does 'to give up smoking' mean 'to stop smoking'?	☐	☐
2 Nowadays, do some people feel very strongly about smokers?	☐	☐
3 Does 'coming round' in the second paragraph mean the same as 'visiting'?	☐	☐

		YES	NO
4	The advice in the third paragraph is for those people who 'find it difficult to get through the day without a cigarette'. Does this mean they will probably have smoked a cigarette by the end of the day?	☐	☐
5	If you smoke and are trying to stop, are you advised to make changes in what you do every day?	☐	☐
6	Once you have decided to stop smoking, are you advised to choose a time and then never smoke from that time on?	☐	☐
7	To help you to stop smoking, are you advised to cut your cigarettes into smaller pieces?	☐	☐
8	If you were a smoker and then you do without, will you be able to carry on your daily life as usual?	☐	☐
9	Is the temptation talked about in the last paragraph the temptation to throw away all your cigarettes?	☐	☐
10	In the last paragraph, does 'give up' mean the same as 'stop'?	☐	☐

EXERCISE THREE

Complete the following paragraph using words from the list below. There is one word for each gap and each word in the list can be used only once. Check you answers with the Key.

getting	fell	~~got~~	get	gets	drawing	get	got	get	get	~~fallen~~
come	~~comes~~	cutting	go	ahead	~~up~~	on	through	out	along	
on	with	behind	back	round	for	~~into~~	out	~~across~~	along	

Young actor Alfred Ferrier is approaching his thirtieth birthday, and to judge by his past decade he can look forward to another decade of success.

Fred **Comes across** as a flamboyant, happy-go-lucky character but he can _____ _____ with the occasional perceptive comment that reveals the more serious side to his character. However, it is the happy-go-lucky side of his character that has given him the reputation for _____ **into** trouble. He tells of the time when he _____ _____ Sue (now his ex-wife) — she was then starring opposite him in the film 'Say it Twice'. He asked her to _____ _____ to his flat for dinner. For the evening's entertainment they tried to see how many night clubs they could get into for free. The police caught up with them in the early morning and they had to spend the next day behind bars before being allowed to go home. When they _____ _____ to the film set two days later they were engaged to be married, but because of that little escapade

19

filming had ~~fallen~~ _____ by two weeks. In spite of his talent for trouble, it is difficult not to _____ _____ with Fred. 'Yes,' he says, 'I _____ _____ _____ most people. I believe in _____ _____ all the pretence in a relationship and I really like to _____ _____ to people's innermost feelings. Mind you, I may not like what I find!'

And what about his recent success? A show on Broadway, an extensive tour, various contracts for television, and all this in the last year. The unkind would say that he _gets_ _____ on charm and good looks rather than _____ _____ any true acting ability. But someone who comes from Stoke Newington, who is _got_ _up_ in a silk bow tie, and who can still _____ _____, must have something more than charm.

EXERCISE FOUR

There are some words missing from the sentences below. Use the missing words to complete the puzzle.

1 The old lady _____ her pet dog back by offering a reward to the finder.

2 Manufactured clothing is of such bad quality nowadays that buttons _____ off and the seams split after only a few days' wear.

3 During the maintenance work the electricity was _____ off.

4 Those two have _____ out because he saw her with another man.

5 He _____ up his free time to instruct his star pupil.

6 He did not see what the comment had to _____ with what they had been discussing.

7 He refused to be _____ into the argument on nuclear disarmament.

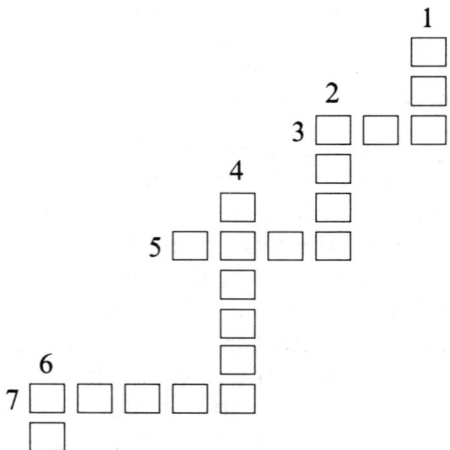

EXERCISE FIVE

In the following text the writer is discussing the increasing problem of personal debt. Do you think that the writer feels sympathetic towards most people in debt? Read the text and check your answer with the Key. Then, read the text again and answer the questions below.

Debt is becoming a huge social problem with credit cards being so easily available, and some of the worst hit are elderly people. Many elderly people would rather do without than get into debt, but an unexpected emergency or death of a partner is far more likely to cause debt than foolish spending.

Money is a very personal thing to talk about and many people do not like to share their financial problems. It would be nice to think that we could always fall back on the support of our family and friends but more often than not we come across the view that if you have got into a mess, you have to get yourself out. But if you have drawn on all your life savings, and have cut your cost of living down to the barest minimum and you are still falling behind on payment of bills, the only way to get out of the situation is to find outside help.

Luckily, there are many groups in Britain that can offer advice. The main way that these groups can help is to draw up a personal budget that can advise the debtor on how to cut back spending to a minimum. They can also come up with recommendations as to the best way to pay back the debt. All these advisory groups are anxious to get across the idea that people must come round to acknowledging their debts far sooner than they do. In this way help can come before the crisis, not after.

1 When the text says 'elderly people would rather do without', what would they not be doing?

2 What is a phrasal verb that means the opposite of 'getting into?'

3 When you fall back on the support of someone, what do you want them to do?

4 What is the usual opinion of family and friends about a person in debt?

5 If you have drawn on all your life savings, how much money do you have left?

6 If you cut your cost of living down, are you still spending some money, and why?

7 If you have cut your cost of living down but you are still falling behind with payments, what can you do?

8 What help can a debt advisory group offer?

9 Are the advisory groups anxious that people in debt visit them?

Read this note. It is from a cleaning lady, Mrs Phelps, to her employer. Mrs Phelps has written the note very informally, as if she was speaking. Rewrite the note so that it is very formal, using words that are more suitable for written language. One way of doing this is by replacing phrasal verbs with non-phrasal verbs. There is a model answer in the Key.

Dear Mr Robinson,

I am writing this note because I have a complaint and my husband says I must come out with it straight.

I would be very happy if you would do away with your dog. I have been doing for you for 9 years now but the trouble I am having with your new dog is getting me down. It gets at all your house plants, it tears the chairs to bits and the creature smells — the pong makes me come over all queasy. Yesterday was the last straw, it came at me in the kitchen for no apparent reason.

Usually I would just get on with my work but I am finding the work too much. I hope that we won't fall out over this but if nothing is done I shall have to give in my notice.

Edna Phelps (Mrs)

Section Three: Part One

EXERCISE ONE

Read the following sentences. Think carefully about the word order and whether the verb is separable or inseparable. Some of the sentences are correct and some are incorrect. Put a tick (√) in the box by the sentences that are correct. Put a cross (×) in the box by the sentences that are incorrect. Check your answers with the Key.

1 Once you have started a course of study it is best to go through with it. ☐

2 The students had to hand their essays by the end of the week in. ☐

3 When he sat his final examination he had gone two nights' sleep without. ☐

4 He kept at his studies until he got his degree, then he said that he would never study again. ☐

5 Her bad headaches made it difficult for her to keep up with the lectures. ☐

6 My friend is so clumsy; when he goes to the library he is always knocking off the books the shelves. ☐

7 When he did so badly in the last exam, it knocked him back. ☐

8 The lecturer refused to let any information out about the next day's exam paper. ☐

EXERCISE TWO

The following text gives advice to students about writing an essay from lecture notes. How many points of advice are given? Read the text and check your answer with the Key.

Writing an essay from lecture notes needs careful organisation. First of all, go over your notes and decide on the main points that you will need to answer the question or to make the argument. If there are any points that you do not understand, go through them with a teacher or with a friend because it will be easy to tell from your essay if there are some points that you do not understand. Do not be tempted to include all the information you have gathered; you must leave out anything that is irrelevant.

Once you have decided which points are relevant to your essay, you need to make a plan; some people find it useful to lay out their ideas in diagram form. When you are satisfied that the points of the plan hang together well, you can then begin to write the essay. Although there will be some points that are easier to write about than others, do not hold forth on one particular point – it is important to keep the discussion of all points as balanced as possible.

As a final piece of advice, make sure that your handwriting doesn't let you down. There is no point in handing in a brilliant essay if your teacher cannot read it.

When you have read the text, underline all the phrasal verbs. Circle the nouns that are directly related to each phrasal verb and draw arrows from the nouns to the verb. Check your answers with the Key.

Examples: (He) was very anxious not to be left out of any (discussion.)
If (you) do not have the time, leave out the political (references.)

EXERCISE THREE

The sentences below are incomplete. Study the sentences and decide what *kind* of word is needed to complete each sentence: a verb, or a phrasal verb particle, or a noun, or an adjective, or an adverb. Write down the kind of word needed in the box at the end of each sentence. Check your answers with the Key.

Example: The traffic was held up by (annoying/a herd of cows/across) crossing the road.

noun

1 He has gone (totally/rebelled/a rebel) against his parents.

2 He believes that old-fashioned (certainly/morals/against) have gone out completely.

3 In his spare time he goes (in/artistic/the paint) for spraying graffiti on walls.

4 His mother doesn't like to go on about (unkindly/ talked/his appearance).

5 He hangs about (off/looking/lazy) for trouble.

6 He (couldn't/the teenager/distressed) hold back his tears when the police questioned him.

7 All the gang hang together against (older/closely/the police)

8 They (unkind/brutally/over) knocked the old woman down and then ran away.

9 The sergeant felt that the major had laid (the soldier/down/selflessly) his life unnecessarily.

10 He laid his (new/into/wearing) jacket carefully aside, rolled up his sleeves and then punched the man on the nose.

When you have decided what kind of word is needed to complete each sentence, look at the list of words given in brackets. Choose the correct word and complete the sentence.

Example: The traffic was held up by (annoying/a herd of cows/across) crossing the road

EXERCISE FOUR

The sentences below are incomplete. Look at the list of items on the right hand side. Which of these items can be used to complete the sentences? (There may be more than one choice.) Circle your answer and then check the Key.

1 There's a rumour going about

    (a) .
    (b) that he is getting divorced.
    (c) Sally.
    (d) concerning the doctor.

2 The scientist went about

    (a) his work.
    (b) so that he could finish in time.
    (c) .
    (d) the experiment in a logical manner.

3 Forty days went by

    (a) and he still wasn't dead.
    (b) so she contacted the police.
    (c) .
    (d) the desert.

4 He knew his way back because he went by

> (a) the stars.
> (b) .
> (c) so that he could see her.
> (d) and brought a map.

5 They hoped the rain would hold off

> (a) .
> (b) for the festival.
> (c) all day.
> (d) the week.

6 The army held off

> (a) .
> (b) the surprise attack.
> (c) bravely.
> (d) the enemy.

7 It was eight o'clock before we knocked off

> (a) .
> (b) for the night.
> (c) so that we could go home.
> (d) the work.

8 He was so clumsy that he knocked off

> (a) the head.
> (b) apologised.
> (c) .
> (d) so that he could get out.

How could you add an adverb to the following sentences? Which of the numbered places would be most suitable for the adverb in brackets?

9 ¹He²knocked³back⁴six pints of lager⁵ (quickly)

10 ¹He²had³knocked⁴about⁵all over the world⁶ (aimlessly)

11 ¹The lion tamer²held³the lion⁴off⁵ (expertly)

12 ¹We²should³hold⁴to⁵our original plan⁶ (definitely)

EXERCISE FIVE

Rewrite the following paragraph in the passive wherever possible. Remember that some phrasal verbs are intransitive and cannot therefore be used in the passive. Check your answers with the Key.

All this happened a few years ago, when I was a young lad and I had just started work at the factory. A friend of mine had managed to lay aside a small amount of gelignite from work and had put it in a small disused shed at the bottom of my father's garden. We wanted to use it to go fishing in the river. One day we had knocked off work early because it was a half-day holiday and we ran to the shed in great excitement. We had conveniently forgotten how the boss had held forth on the dangers of explosives. We just hoped that the rain would keep off for our fishing trip. We were going down my father's garden when all of a sudden, with no warning, there was an almighty bang and the whole shed went up in smoke. The explosion knocked us over but we recovered and ran back up the garden, only to find my father standing there. As can be imagined, he was furious and demanded a full explanation. In the end my father let us off lightly because he never let on to our boss that we had taken some explosives.

In the sentences below, change the noun phrases in brackets to pronouns where possible, *without changing the order of the words*. Remember the rules for the position of the object pronoun.

1 (The lawyer) can't go back on (his word).

2 (The boy) handed back (the car keys).

3 Parents must learn to hold (their tempers) in.

4 It is a good idea to keep in with (the neighbours).

5 The company laid off (300 men).

6 You need to lay off (the chocolate).

EXERCISE SIX

Using each of the sentences below to help you, make new sentences by replacing the phrases in brackets with grammatically correct phrases of your own. Check the Key for model answers.

Example: The dog kept on (trying to get back into the house).

The dog kept on barking throughout the night.

1 (The villain) went back on (his word).

2 The prisoner went without (food for three weeks).

3 (The husband) went over (the past events) again and again.

4 (The farmer) handed over (the gun to the police for inspection).

5 (As the climber spun round and round), he grimly held onto (the rope).

6 (The park keepers) kept shouting at the children (to keep off the grass).

7 (The boys) kept out of trouble (to avoid further punishment).

8 (After he had got home from the office, Andrew) knocked back a large whisky.

9 (The cook) had laid aside (all the necessary ingredients).

10 (Slimmers have to) lay off the cream cakes.

11 The passenger left (his raincoat) behind on the train.

12 (The mother) felt that she had been let down by (all her children).

Section Three: Part Two

EXERCISE ONE

Read the following sentences. There is a short list of verbs accompanying each sentence. From the list, find the verb that is the closest in meaning to the underlined verb in the sentence. Circle your answer and then check the Key.

1 She <u>went about</u> her daily business as if she wasn't being observed.

> circulated
> accompanied
> tackled
> visited

2 He <u>went along with</u> their plan because he knew that he had no choice.

> walked
> cooperated with
> looked at
> proceeded

3 Modern technology has enabled us to find the exact spot where the famous ship, the Titanic, <u>went down</u>.

> sank
> fell
> was received
> set

4 He <u>went through</u> the newspaper to find the article he wanted.

> used
> searched through
> suffered
> completed

5 The information sheets were <u>handed out</u> before the lecture so that the students would have time to study them.

> distributed
> submitted
> returned
> delivered

6 The different parts of the film <u>hung together</u> to make a very believable story.

> suspended
> were consistent
> supported each other
> ended simultaneously

7 All evening he <u>held forth</u> on his favourite subject, cruelty to donkeys, and bored all the other guests.

> talked endlessly
> went forward
> withheld
> continued

8 The water supply would <u>hold out</u> for one month. After that they would face certain death.

> resist
> wait
> postpone
> last

9 The information was <u>kept back</u> by the government, supposedly for the public's own good.

withheld
delayed
concealed
repressed

10 If you <u>keep to</u> your part of the agreement, I will keep to mine.

maintain
adhere to
continue
retain

11 It is doubtful whether salaries can <u>keep up with</u> inflation.

delay
continue
maintain in good condition
keep pace with

12 The price of the picture was <u>knocked down</u> as the artist wanted a quick sale.

struck
reduced
demolished
auctioned

13 She <u>laid aside</u> some of her best linen for when her daughter got married.

saved
placed to one side
abandoned
sacrificed

14 They <u>left</u> the outside lights <u>on</u> so that their visitors could easily find their way.

missed
didn't switch off
left in position
disregarded

15 He felt <u>let down</u> when his brother didn't keep his appointment.

lowered
disappointed
depressed
involved

EXERCISE TWO

The following text gives instructions on how to make a soft toy. From this list, choose which things you have to do to make the toy:

embroider	paint	cut out	glue	sew	knit	stuff

Read the text and check your answers with the Key.

> In last week's magazine we saw how easy it was to make a child's dress from a simple pattern. This week, because of overwhelming demand, we shall have a look at how to make a small stuffed toy. This pattern is so simple you could probably make this adorable little rabbit in a morning.

You will need about half a metre of synthetic fur. Go for the material that has the British Standard safety mark on it because it is less flammable and easier to wash. You will also need half a kilo of kapok for stuffing and some pieces of coloured felt for the eyes and tongue. Once you have assembled all the materials, go through the instructions carefully. Lay the pattern out on the cloth, making sure that the long pieces do not go against the nap (the direction of the cloth's fibres). Hold the pattern in place with pins and then cut out the pieces; it is best to leave the pattern on the material until you begin to sew. Follow the sewing directions carefully, making sure that you leave enough gaps to put the stuffing in. When you have finished sewing, turn the toy inside out and pull it into shape. Then stuff the toy with kapok, using a pencil to push the stuffing into the ears and legs. Keep the stuffing in with your fingers as you sew the toy up. To finish the toy, cut out shapes for the eyes and tongue, stitch them on and embroider a nose and mouth as shown in the picture.

I am sure that this pattern will not let you down, especially when you see the expression of delight on the face of the child you give it to.

The statements below are about the text. Are they correct or incorrect? Put a tick (√) in the box for correct statements. Put a cross (×) in the box for incorrect statements.

1 You should choose material that has a British Standard safety mark on it. ☐

2 You need not read the instructions carefully. ☐

3 The cloth should be put on the pattern. ☐

4 The long pieces of the pattern should follow the direction of the fur fibres. ☐

5 You should pin the pattern on to the cloth. ☐

6 The pattern should remain on the cloth while you cut out the pieces. ☐

7 The stuffing will not come out as you sew because the material is pinned together. ☐

8 The writer thinks that you will not be disappointed with the result. ☐

EXERCISE THREE

Complete the following paragraph using words from the list below. There is one word for each gap and each word in the list can be used only once. Check your answers with the Key.

go	holding	laid	kept	~~let~~	kept	go	let	~~off~~	for	back
	~~ahead~~	on	down	about	in	at	for			

When a leading potato crisp manufacturer closed down its factory in Scotland, it was seen as a challenge to the determined workforce and the local management. Dennis Pringle, the managing director of the present firm, commented, 'We first knew the company wanted to close the factory when men were being _____ _off_ unnecessarily and the management in London _____ _____ _____ the lack of markets in Scotland. When the closure was formally announced, we all felt we had been _____ _____, but we were determined to keep the factory open and so we went independent. We didn't realise what we had _let_ ourselves _____ _____ but because everyone concerned _____ _____ it, our business has been a major success. After we had decided to _____ _ahead_ independently, we had to raise all our own financial backing, but now we've started there's no _____ us _____. Our Highland crisps are well-known now and we are continually expanding our markets – in America they particularly _____ _____ our new range of crisps, Dennis the Menace Mean Streaks.'

EXERCISE FOUR

Read the sentences below. Complete the word puzzle using verbs – in the infinitive – that have the same meaning as the underlined words in the sentences.

1 I'll go along with you part of the way.

2 You go ahead, I'll catch up with you later.

3 The dog went after the cat.

4 I'll eat whatever is left over.

5 Why did she leave all the scandal out of her autobiography?

6 I wish you would keep from mentioning her ex-husband.

7 If you go on eating like that, you'll get fat.

8 He hung back as he felt too shy to speak to her.

9 Because he was upset, he went about his work in a very half-hearted way.

```
    9
1 ☐ ☐ ☐ ☐ ☐ ☐ ☐ ☐ ☐
2 ☐ ☐ ☐ ☐ ☐ ☐ ☐
3 P U R S U E
4 ☐ ☐ ☐ ☐ ☐ ☐
5 ☐ ☐ ☐ ☐
6 ☐ ☐ ☐ ☐ ☐
7 ☐ ☐ ☐ ☐ ☐ ☐ ☐ ☐
8 ☐ ☐ ☐ ☐ ☐ ☐ ☐ ☐
```

EXERCISE FIVE

The following text describes part of the life of an actor, Arthur Bottomly. How old is Arthur? Do you think he is under 30, or between 30 and 40, or between 40 and 50, or over 50? Read the text and check your answer with the Key. Then read the text again and answer the questions below.

Arthur Bottomly has recently finished a successful tour with a major theatre company. Our correspondent went round to his charming cottage in Surrey to talk to him.

Once Arthur starts talking about his early life he holds forth at great length on the delights and cosiness of his working-class background, obviously not wanting to go into the rather more painful and uncomfortable moments as the son of an out-of-work bus driver and an alcoholic mother, being brought up on the seventeenth floor of a tower block. He says that seventeen has always been his lucky number.

When he was very young he remembers hanging around the dressing rooms of the local theatre company. 'The actors and actresses never used to take much notice of a small lad of twelve. I even used to get a few hand-me-downs from Ed Warnsley to take home to my father.' As soon as he was old enough, he started to work for the theatre, doing whatever jobs he could get. His talent was soon recognised and he was given some good parts. He found that he could leave behind his past and enter a world where money was easily made and easily spent. He realises that he very foolishly never laid aside any money from this time. Then the theatre went bankrupt and all the actors were laid off. He met his wife, Sally Cooper, at this time. 'By gosh we've been through some hard times together,' he remembers. She was wardrobe mistress for the same company and was made redundant at the same time as Arthur. When Arthur had to leave the area to find work where he could, he had to leave Sally behind because she was looking after her sick father. She says, 'We've hung together all these years. I've never wanted to keep him back. He never lays down the law to me and he's always respected my decisions. I think that's a very strong basis for a relationship.'

After they had got married, Arthur knocked about doing pantomime for a couple of years but he always kept up with his serious acting. 'I love serious drama and although it is a cliché, I long to play the lead in *Macbeth*. When I do a serious piece of drama I feel that I can lay aside my troubles and live in another world.' His first big break came when he was offered a leading part in a touring company performance. From there he has never looked back.

And the future, what does it hold? 'I'm going to keep at my serious acting for a while. If I don't succeed, I'll probably go in for television. They seem to like character actors there and I have been told I'm the kind of character they can use.' And with such a likeable character as Arthur Bottomly, who can question that?

1 How was the information for this article collected?

2 What parts of his early childhood does Arthur like to talk about?

3 What parts of his early childhood does Arthur not like to talk about?

4 What was Arthur's first contact with the theatre?

5 When Arthur started his first jobs in the theatre, what did he do with the money that he earned?

6 Why were times hard for Sally and Arthur when they first met?

7 What makes a strong basis for a relationship, according to Sally?

8 Was Arthur serious about acting in pantomime?

9 What kind of acting does Arthur prefer, and why?

10 What plans does Arthur have for his future acting career?

EXERCISE SIX

Rewrite the sentences below in a more informal way using one phrasal verb from the following list for each sentence. You should also try to replace as many formal words and phrases with informal ones as possible. There are several ways of doing this. Check the Key for model answers.

go in for	go through with	hold out	keep on about	let off
leave off	hang together	go about with	go back on	hang onto
keep in with	knock about	lay out	let in for	hand back

Example: Ladies and gentlemen, I am delighted to announce that the time has come for you to stop work.

Ok. everyone, I am very happy to say you can knock off now

1 I wish you would refrain from keeping company with such undesirable people.

2 He has adopted bee-keeping as a hobby.

3 I am quite distressed that he has failed to keep his word.

4 He feels that he cannot complete the course due to its unforeseen difficulty.

5 I am retaining possession of my company shares until the appropriate selling time.

6 Ladies and gentlemen, we must all support one another in these difficult times.

7 You must continue to resist his advances until he makes a proposal of marriage.

8 I should be grateful if you would return the key to the receptionist.

9 You ought to remain friendly with Lady Maxwell as she is married to the general.

10 I wish you would not continually talk about your flying experiences. We have heard them many times before.

11 He has wandered about here and there seeing the world.

12 We had to spend a fortune to make our daughter's wedding a splendid occasion.

13 I wish the two of you would cease your interminable bickering.

14 He is going to be very annoyed as she has involved him in selling cakes at the church fête.

15 The children were excused early from school today.

Section Four: Part One

EXERCISE ONE

Read the following sentences. Think carefully about the word order and whether the verb is separable or inseparable. Some of the sentences are correct and some are incorrect. Put a tick (√) in the box by the sentences that are correct. Put a cross (×) in the box by the sentences that are incorrect. Check your answers with the Key.

1 They looked all the application forms at before coming to a decision. ☐

2 He thought there was nothing wrong with making up some of his references when he applied for the job. ☐

3 The job satisfaction made partly up for the low salary. ☐

4 The chance of promotion passed him by because of his prison record. ☐

5 The accountant pays out the wages on a Thursday afternoon. ☐

6 It was raining so he put on his hat and pulled down it over his ears. ☐

7 Although he thought his ideas were right, he was so nervous that he had great difficulty in putting across them. ☐

8 He certainly won't get a good job now. He's run off with the Director General's daughter. ☐

EXERCISE TWO

The following text discusses the fortunes of a football team, United. What adjectives are used to give a positive description? Read the text and check your answers with the Key.

In the summer of this year, James Griffiths, the United manager, was having great difficulty in putting together a strong team for the forthcoming season. Now, months later, the team's recent performance has more than made up for the earlier difficulties. The gamble to pay a quarter of a million pounds for full-back Ian Hogg has paid off. This player combines skilful manoeuvring with brilliant strategy, and the combination of Hogg with the three young unknowns, Higgins, Scott and MacArthur, has resulted in a team that can produce championship football without too much effort.

Last weekend saw them making away with their sixth win of the season. It was a game that their opponents, City, had to put down to experience as they soon found that they had run up against some serious competition. In the first half, Archie Ogilvy scored a brilliant goal by ploughing through the feeble City defence. Once exposed by Ogilvy, none of the tough forwards let one opportunity pass by to take advantage of this weakness and they slammed home another two goals before half time.

For the remainder of the match, City were pulled down by their lack of stamina and although the United winger, Stewart Cotton, fell and put out his shoulder, United won 6–1. We are all looking forward to the match next week, when United meet second-placed Albion. This will be a match that will really sort out the men from the boys.

When you have read the text, underline all the phrasal verbs. Circle the nouns that are directly related to each phrasal verb and draw arrows from the nouns to the verb. Check your answers with the Key.

Examples: (Scott) ran after the (ball.)

        This (match) went a long way towards <u>making up</u> for their appalling (record.)

EXERCISE THREE

The sentences below are incomplete. Study the sentences and decide what *kind* of word is needed to complete each sentence: a verb, or a phrasal verb particle, or a noun, or an adjective, or an adverb. Write down the kind of word needed in the box at the end of each sentence. Check your answers with the Key.

Example: He put on a (boy/surprised/beautifully) expression, but he actually knew all about it.
     | adjective |

1 He was looking after (carefully/the cat/with) all that week.
     | |

2 Their house looks (the garden/lovely/directly) onto the park.
     | |

3 His generous nature made up (for/completely/angry) his temper.
     | |

4 It started to rain. They saw the bus shelter so they (made/fast/very) quickly for it.
     | |

5 Dolores cut up the pie and put aside (nicely/tasty/a piece) for Harry, who was coming home late.

6 He's got to see a doctor. He mustn't put it (delayed/off/illness) any longer.

7 I don't know why he puts up with such (difficulty/thankless/around) work.

8 His hat blew off so he had to (fast/run/wind) after it.

9 He has (foolishly/been/after) run off with his boss's daughter.

10 The dog had been run (soon/horribly/over) by a lorry.

When you have decided what kind of word is needed to complete each sentence, look at the list of words given in brackets. Choose the correct word and complete the sentence.

Example: He put on a (~~boy~~/surprised/~~beautifully~~) expression, but he actually knew all about it.

EXERCISE FOUR

Look at the sentences below. Which sentences would be grammatically correct without the phrase in brackets and which would be incorrect without the phrase in brackets? Remember that some phrasal verbs are transitive — they must be followed by an object. For your answers underline the phrases that can be omitted and then check the Key.

Example: The train pulled into (the station).
It was midnight when the train pulled in (and the film star arrived).

1 When he apologised for his mistake, he looked away (in embarrassment).

2 A taxi pulled up (opposite the hotel).

3 He put forward (his idea at last night's meeting).

4 He looks down on (people who come from the Copthorne area of town).

5 When the boys saw the old lady come to the window, they made off (down the alleyway).

6 She said she would pay back (the money as soon as she sold her flat).

7 The rain was so heavy that he couldn't make out (the distant hills).

8 She made up to (him hoping to get a promotion).

9 His grandfather passed away (on Tuesday night).

10 She put off (going to the dentist until her toothache was very bad).

11 Although he is English, he could easily pass for (an Italian because he has lived in Italy for twenty years).

12 In spite of their differences, they pulled together (to get the report finished on time).

13 The soldier lay dying, run through (the neck with a bayonet).

14 The children were told to run along (to the shops).

15 They looked at (several houses before deciding to buy Rose Cottage).

Where possible in the following sentences, change the noun phrases in brackets to pronouns *without changing the order of the words.* Remember that the particle of a separable phrasal verb must follow an object pronoun.

Example: (The written exam) pulled down (his marks).

It pulled down his marks. NOT *It pulled down them.*

16 (The manager) refused to look at (the report).

17 (The walkers) were looking out for (the rare plant).

18 (The visitor) wanted to look up (his old friend).

19 The cloud was so thick (the mountain climbers) couldn't make out (the summit).

20 (The student) promised to pay (his father) back.

21 (The child) ran across (the road) without looking.

How could you add an adverb to the following sentences? Which of the numbered places would be most suitable for the adverb in brackets?

22 ^{1}He^{2}looked^{3}round^{4}to see who was there. (quickly)

23 ^{1}Her grandfather^{2}passed^{3}away^{4}last night^5. (quietly)

24 ^{1}The charity^{2}pays^{3}out^{4}to those in need^5. (regularly)

25 ^{1}The volunteer had been^{2}put^{3}through^{4}the terrible ordeal^5. (unnecessarily)

26 ^{1}She^{2}ran^{3}off^{4}with^{5}her lover^6. (secretly)

EXERCISE FIVE

Where possible, rewrite the following sentences in the passive. Remember that some phrasal verbs are intransitive and cannot therefore be used in the passive. Check your answers with the Key.

Example: The editor ran through the script.

The script was run through by the editor.

38

1 He looked away in shame when he was questioned.

2 His aunt made over the business to his trustees.

3 Muriel can pass for a Spaniard.

4 The debtor paid the money back in instalments.

5 The demolition team pulled the old house down.

6 The car pulled over to let the ambulance pass.

7 The shop assistant put aside the best bargains for her mother.

8 The taxi put me down at the station.

9 The projectionist ran the film back.

10 The water ran over the edge of the tank.

Make sentences using the words given below. (The words may not be in the correct order). Remember the rules for the position of the object pronoun.

Example: (a) The dog / the cat / ran / after

The dog ran after the cat.

(b) It / it / ran / after

It ran after it.

11 (a) Her nephew / the fortune / ran / through
(b) He / it / ran / through

12 (a) The technician / the tape / ran / through
(b) She / it / ran / through

13 (a) The queen / the hotel / passed / by
(b) She / it / passed / by

14 (a) The politician / the comment / passed / by
(b) He / it / passed / by

15 (a) The manageress / the young waiter / looked / up and down
(b) She / him / looked / up and down

16 (a) The boy / his hero / looked / up to
(b) He / him / looked / up to

EXERCISE SIX

Using each of the sentences below to help you, make new sentences by replacing the phrases in brackets with grammatically correct phrases of your own. Check the Key for model answers.

Example: (With the help of his comrades) he pulled through his fever.

Medical help came at last so he pulled through his fever.

1 She had looked after (her elderly mother for years).

2 I am looking forward to (hearing from you in due course).

3 (The thief quietly) passed by (the open window).

4 (With his black hair and fluent Arabic) he could easily pass for (an Arab).

5 (He didn't have any money so) he paid her back (in stamps).

6 The call was put through (to the office in New York).

7 She put him off because (she wanted to keep her weekend free).

8 Her boss kept putting her down because (he couldn't stand pushy women).

9 She quickly put the cat down (because it smelt).

10 (The car took four months) to run in.

11 (The waiter saw a customer had left her purse) and immediately ran after her.

12 (Before the exam) the teacher quickly ran through (all the questions).

Section Four: Part Two

Match each of the expressions below to one of the following cartoons. Write the number of the expression next to the letter of the cartoon, e.g. (e)4. Check your answers with the Key.

1 Look it over.
2 Put that away!
3 Kiss and make up.
4 Pass it on.
5 Make for the beach!
6 Pull up.
7 Look out!
8 Run along.
9 Put that out!
10 Pay up.

EXERCISE TWO

The following text gives advice on how to choose the best bank for your needs. Which bank services are mentioned in the text? Read the text and check your answers with the Key.

When you are looking around for the best bank for your needs, it is a good idea to make sure that the bank you choose offers a certain range and quality of service. You have to remember that when a bank looks after your money, it is also looking after your future.

When you start to look into all the facts and figures supplied by the bank, you shouldn't be put off by the financial and legal language. If you don't understand something, ask for a clearer explanation; it is your right to know how your money is being used and it is the bank's duty to explain clearly.

Remember to check on the rates of bank charges and you will need to look out for the rates of interest on borrowed money. Once you have opened an account, find out about the different ways that you can pay into it. Ask the bank whether you can pay off bills by all the usual means, e.g. standing order, direct debit, budget payment, etc. Make sure that you know how to make out a cheque correctly and find out how often the bank makes up statements.

Good relations with your bank are important; you never know when you might want to put down a deposit in a hurry or when you might run up against an emergency. Honesty from you will ensure cash and cooperation from your bank.

Are the statements below correct or incorrect? Put a tick (√) in the box for correct statements or a cross (×) for incorrect statements.

1 This text gives advice to people who are searching for a bank to use. ☐

2 A bank cares indirectly for your future. ☐

3 You should visit the bank's facts and figures. ☐

4 You will be disturbed by the facts and figures. ☐

5 The text advises you to be aware of the rates of interest on borrowed money. ☐

6 '. . . different ways that you can pay into it.' 'It' means the bank. ☐

7 To 'pay off bills' means to send them by post. ☐

8 To make out a cheque you need a pen. ☐

9 Banks invent statements. ☐

10 Banks can help you if you meet with an emergency. ☐

42

EXERCISE THREE

Read the following questions.

1 Did he regard the major with contempt?

2 Did he turn away from her?

3 Will he abscond with my money?

4 Will that dog attack me?

5 Did you withdraw money from this account?

6 Was the express train entering the station?

7 Did that company erect the building?

8 Did you switch the lights on?

9 Did the old lady flee from her attackers?

10 Did he remove his gloves?

Now answer each question in the negative. For your answers use a phrasal verb that means the opposite of the main verb in each question. You will need the following phrasal verbs:

put off	**put on**	**look up to**	**pay back**	**run away**
run after	**pull down**	**look at**	**pay in**	**pull out**

Example: Did she gaze at herself in the mirror?

No, she looked away.

EXERCISE FOUR

The verbs are missing from the sentences below. Use the missing words to complete the puzzle, working clockwise. In the puzzle, each of the verbs borrows the last letter of the verb in front and the first letter of the verb after.

Example: makeupassover_undown

1 How could you _____ _____ a chance to travel abroad, just because your cat's ill?

2 He _____ _____ his idea so well that everybody was convinced.

3 Why do you _____ _____ that man? I know he's good looking but he's not worth the effort.

4 Come to my house on Thursday and we'll _____ _____ the plan together.

5 The milkman is going to _____ _____ Member of Parliament.

6 Whenever you go shopping, you _____ _____ an enormous bill at the tailor's.

7 You ought to _____ _____ as you did the damage.

8 _____ _____ at the next petrol station as the tank's nearly empty.

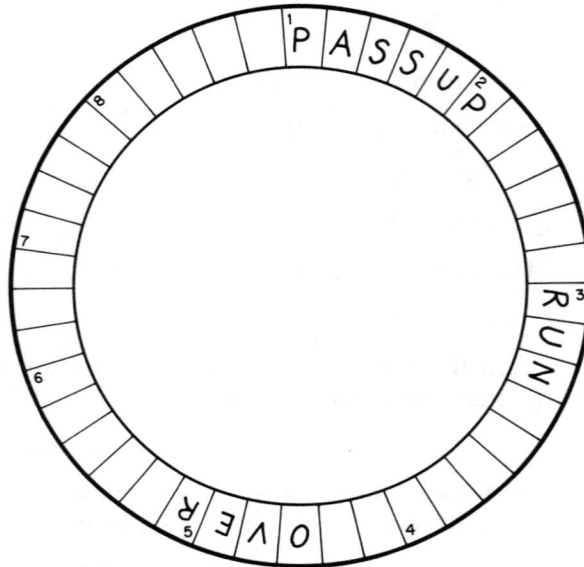

EXERCISE FIVE

The following text is part of a fictional story. What kind of story could it have come from — a romance, a detective story, a thriller, a ghost story, an historical novel? Read the text and check your answer with the Key. Read the text again and then answer the questions below.

> Clark sat slumped in his chair in the café, idly stirring his black coffee. He was trying to think, but nothing made sense any more; the espionage game had become far more tangled and complicated than in the years of the Cold War. He was hoping that Jim would look in soon and answer some questions.
>
> He heard the tap, tap, tap of approaching footsteps. He looked up and saw a woman, heavily made up, expensively dressed, walking along the pavement towards the café. She passed by, seemingly not noticing the admiring stares she attracted. There was something about her that made Clark look a second time. The way she clutched her bag under her arm, the quick steps

44

she was taking, the way she kept looking round — she was a frightened woman.

A black sedan, parked across the road from the café, started its engine and pulled out from the sidewalk into the road, but then it began to slow down. Clark's instincts told him something was wrong. He leapt out of his chair and ran after the woman. The car was almost alongside, when Clark, panting, grabbed hold of the woman's arm and pulled her away from the kerb. Her frightened eyes bulged, her mouth opened, but she made no sound. The black sedan suddenly revved up and made off down the street.

Clark held onto the woman's arm, supporting her as she collapsed against him.

'Do you know who those guys were?' he asked. But he got no answer — the woman had passed out.

1 Who was Clark hoping for a visit from?

2 Why did Clark have to look up to see the woman?

3 What did the woman have on her face?

4 What place did the woman go past?

5 In what direction did the woman look that told Clark she was frightened?

6 What position did the black sedan leave when it started off?

7 Why did Clark chase the woman?

8 How did Clark get the woman out of danger?

9 How do we know that Clark was right to suspect the people in the car of trying to harm the woman?

10 Was the woman conscious when Clark began to ask questions?

EXERCISE SIX

The conversation below is between a student and his teacher. It is a very formal conversation. Read the conversation then rewrite it as if you were the student reporting it very informally to a friend. The first part has been done for you.

Teacher: I've been examining your essay on 'Fluid Mechanics'. I'm afraid I am rather disappointed. To start with, your writing is so bad that I had the greatest difficulty in deciphering it.

Student: I'm sorry. I was away playing cricket for the college all last week so I didn't have much time.

Teacher: Young man, you need to devote your energy to more work, not more cricket. I believe you are heading for a high-class degree, but your lack of organisation is weakening your standard. To explain your ideas effectively you need to have good organisation.

Student: I think I exhausted all my ideas in this essay.

Teacher: Is that why you let your imagination take complete control? You should study your lecture notes and read a lot more. You will find that effort will prove profitable in the long run.

Student: Yes, thank you, sir.

My teacher told me he had been looking at my essay...

Section Five: Part One

EXERCISE ONE

Read the following sentences. Think carefully about the word order and whether the verb is separable or inseparable. Some of the sentences are correct and some are incorrect. Put a tick (✓) in the box by the sentences that are correct. Put a cross (×) in the box by the sentences that are incorrect. Check your answers with the Key.

1 They saw over the house in the morning and by the afternoon they had decided to buy it. ☐

2 The clauses of the contract were set down in difficult legal language. ☐

3 When they first saw the house, it was autumn and the deep golden light of the sun showed off it at its best. ☐

4 They stood around waiting while the agent went to find the key. ☐

5 In the advertisement, 'ch' stands for central heating. ☐

6 He was taken completely aback by the low price of the farmhouse. ☐

7 He took to the building trade like a duck to water. ☐

8 The old lady was worn by the many visitors out interested in buying her house. ☐

EXERCISE TWO

The following paragraph is a description of a certain type of pottery. There are two kinds of pottery vessel described — what are they? Read the paragraph and check your answers with the Key.

In the Han period of Chinese ceramics (206 BC – AD 220), the makers of pottery had not yet worked out a style of their own but copied their pottery styles from bronze vessels. A typical example of this are the Hill Jars, which were made in both pottery and bronze. These jars have conical lids, which stand for the Isle of the Immortals rising above the waves. On the lower part of the jars there is usually a lively decoration of bears, deer, tigers and imaginary monsters all in full gallop. There is also the Taoist Mountain of Paradise always worked into the design. Of the same period are granary urns that show us the shape of the classic Chinese corn barn. These urns are therefore doubly valuable because we are able to see through the craft of pottery into the craft of architecture. If you are thinking of buying a piece of Han pottery for your collection, a 14th century Han bowl could set you back at least $20,000.

When you have read the paragraph, underline all the phrasal verbs. Circle the nouns that are directly related to each phrasal verb and draw arrows from the nouns to the verb. Check your answers with the Key.

Examples: It is best to set about collecting in a systematic way.

The Han period stands out as an exceptional period.

EXERCISE THREE

The sentences below are incomplete. Study the sentences and decide what *kind* of word is needed to complete each sentence: a verb, or a phrasal verb particle, or a noun, or an adjective, or an adverb. Write down the kind of word needed in the box at the end of each sentence. Check your answers with the Key.

Example: She (on/quickly/woman) took down the telephone number.

> adverb

1 Everyone present stood (up/the crowd/standing) when the Queen came in.

2 The grape pickers all (set/quickly/the vines) to as soon as the sun rose.

3 The effects of the transquilliser began to wear (complete/drug/off) a few hours later.

4 He quickly turned the (played/choking/happily) child upside down.

5 The athlete (ran/gradually/track) worked up to eight hours' training a day.

6 He turned down (the offer/rudely/asking) of a lift.

7 He thought (the idea/around/carefully) about the proposal.

8 We saw (go/our visitors/waiting) off at the station.

9 His ignorance (showed/information/against) him up as a fraud.

10 That girl takes after (her mother/completely/beautiful).

When you have decided what kind of word is needed to complete each sentence, look at the list of words given in brackets. Choose the correct word and complete the sentence.

Example: She (~~on~~/quickly/~~woman~~) took down the telephone number.

EXERCISE FOUR

The sentences below are incomplete. Look at the list of items on the right hand side. Which of these items can be used to complete the sentences? (There may be more than one choice.) Circle your answer and then check the Key.

1 I shall have to see to

(a) and book a ticket.
(b) the travel arrangements.
(c) his affairs.
(d) .

2 The butcher set aside

(a) the fatty scraps of meat.
(b) .
(c) his knife.
(d) and talked to the customer.

3 She loved to show off

(a) and sing.
(b) .
(c) her talent for languages.
(d) her daughters.

4 The crowd stood by

(a) and cheered.
(b) watched over by the police.
(c) .
(d) in silence.

5 She couldn't take in

(a) and fainted.
(b) .
(c) the fact she had won the lottery.
(d) the information.

6 Let's all think back

(a) four years.
(b) and remember Harry.
(c) to where we were in 1962.
(d) .

7 I've thrown out

(a) .
(b) my old fur coat.
(c) the broken chair.
(d) and regretted it.

8 They turned away

(a) .
(b) in disgust.
(c) to walk down the path.
(d) and began to talk.

9 The days wore on

(a) and turned into weeks.
(b) and the nights got longer.
(c) .
(d) until he found the courage.

10 Every night she worked on

(a) perfecting her technique.
(b) .
(c) and became an expert.
(d) her language studies.

Where possible in the following sentences, change the noun phrases in brackets to pronouns *without changing the order of the words.* Remember that the particle of a separable phrasal verb must follow an object pronoun.

Example: (The headmaster) would not stand for (rudeness).

He would not stand for it.

11 (The supplies) should see (the winter) out.

12 (The policeman) took down (the address).

13 (The young man) turned against (his family).

14 (Alice) was showing off (her new car).

How could you add an adverb to the following sentences? Which of the numbered places would be most suitable for the adverbs in brackets?

15 ¹The men²stood³about⁴during their lunch break.⁵ (idly)

16 ¹The heels of her shoes were²worn³down.⁴ (completely)

17 ¹The wild deer²stood³out⁴against the sky.⁵ (clearly)

18 ¹Everyone needs to²think³about⁴the future.⁵ (carefully)

EXERCISE FIVE

Where possible, rewrite the following sentences in the passive. Remember that some phrasal verbs are intransitive and cannot therefore be used in the passive. Check your answers with the Key.

Example: Mr Stanley worked out the solution.

The solution was worked out by Mr Stanley.

1 The terrorist set off the bomb.

2 The crowd stood back from the fire.

3 The fireman turned the water on.

4 The nurse took away the glucose drip.

5 Despite the initial problems, everything worked out in the end.

Make sentences using the words given below. (The words may not be in the correct order.) Remember the rules for the position of the object pronoun.

Example: (a) The worker / his rights / stood / up for

The worker stood up for his rights.

(b) He / them / for / stood up

He stood up for them.

6 (a) The lawyer / his client / the hearing / saw / through
(b) He / him / it / saw / through

7 (a) The wife / her husband's promise / saw / through
(b) She / it / saw / through

8 (a) The cook / the oven / turned / on
(b) He / it / turned / on

9 (a) The solution / economic cooperation / turns / on
(b) It / it / turns / on

10 (a) The lecturer / the explanation / was working / up to
(b) He / it / was working / up to

11 (a) The teenage son / his mother / was working / up
(b) He / her / was working / up

Make questions from the following words.

12 do / is / he / think / up / what / to / you /?

13 taken / you / why / aback / were /?

14 do / about / how / you / set / starting /?

15 the offer / turn / he / will / down /?

16 through / you / his motives / can / see /?

EXERCISE SIX

Using each of the sentences below to help you, make new sentences by replacing the phrases in brackets with grammatically correct phrases of your own. Check the Key for model answers.

Example: (It was well past midnight before) we turned in.

After saying goodnight we turned in.

1 She set aside (her knitting to answer the door).

2 (The rules and regulations) were set out (in black and white).

3 We were shown around (by a very entertaining guide).

4 If you like, I shall see to (the catering arrangements).

5 (His ability to lead) set him apart from his fellows.

6 He took the car apart (piece by piece).

7 He took up (freelance security work) when he left the army.

8 The dog was taken out (at least once a day).

9 She asked him what he thought of (the latest fashions).

10 She turned up her collar (against the rain).

11 The maid was so worn out that (she couldn't look after her own family properly).

12 The chemist worked at (the formula all night).

Section Five: Part Two

EXERCISE ONE

Read the following sentences. There is a short list of verbs accompanying each sentence. From the list, find the verb that is the closest in meaning to the underlined verb in the sentence. Circle your answer and then check the Key.

1 She asked if she could <u>see over</u> his yacht.

investigate inspect take care of look at

2 They <u>set aside</u> their differences in opinion because they had to work together.

placed to one side annulled disregarded consolidated

3 The government's plans were <u>set out</u> in no uncertain terms in a recently published report.

displayed stated organised intended

4 Because the interview was live, the leader of the pop group was <u>shown up</u> to be the idiot he really was.

revealed embarrassed displayed arrived

5 Although he was the favourite candidate for the new job, they made him <u>stand down</u> because of his past political activities.

leave be a candidate take the place withdraw

6 We shall <u>stand up for</u> our rights to have political freedom.

rise to defend resist watch

7 It's far easier to <u>take</u> something <u>apart</u> than it is to put it back together again.

put to one side remove dismantle subtract

8 She gave me her address and I <u>took</u> it <u>down</u> but I've lost the piece of paper.

wrote down dismantled was humilated demolished

9 The hospital rang to say that his wife had died in the middle of the night. He was so shocked he just couldn't take it in.

be deceived
receive
understand
comprise

10 He said that he would think about it over the weekend, before coming to any decision.

plan
remember
consider
reflect upon

11 He threw away his last chance to keep his job when he was rude to the manager.

scattered
missed
disposed of
rejected

12 They turned his proposal down because it was going to be too expensive to put into practice.

lowered
rejected
folded
became hostile to

13 In spite of being such a horrible child, he has turned out to be quite a civilised adult.

proved to be
expelled
gathered
extinguished

14 The doctor was confident that the side effects of the drug would wear off after a few days.

remove
weaken
disappear
become useless

15 The marriage didn't work out and they were divorced a year later.

solve
develop well
exhaust
estimate

EXERCISE TWO

The following text is a description of an open-air museum. Where would you find a text like this — on an advertising poster, in a brochure, in a national museum's bulletin, in a history textbook? Read the text and check your answer with the Key.

Any visitor to the north country must set aside a day to see the Buxton Open Air Museum. This is an outing that offers education in its most entertaining form and relaxation at its most enjoyable. There is plenty to see for old and young alike.

The Open Air Museum comprises a reconstructed 19th century mining village, a working farm, a reconstructed coal mine and a museum of social history. All of this is situated on an 80 hectare site in the picturesque valley of the River

Ale. There is also a coffee shop and a children's playground. To see everything at Buxton would easily take up a whole day.

The reconstruction of the mining village took over five years. Various buildings of interest in the area were taken down brick by brick, stone by stone and re-erected on their present site. All the buildings and exhibits that you can see at Buxton have not only been set up to show them off to their best advantage, but also to recreate the feeling and atmosphere of a northern mining village in the 19th century.

A visit to the Museum's working farm will be most enjoyable. You will be able to see original 19th century farm machinery being used, help feed the pigs and goats, ride one of the first tractors ever built, and there are pony rides for children thrown in free of charge.

The mine and the museum of social history have attracted a lot of attention in the past year. They stand out from other museums in the country because of their originality in design. Their success is shown by the fact that they welcome over a million visitors each year.

You can see over Buxton Open Air Museum every day of the year, except Sundays.

Answer the questions below by putting a tick (√) in the box for yes or the box for no.

	YES	NO
1 Are you advised to reserve a day for the Buxton Open Air Museum when you visit the north country?	☐	☐
2 Would it be easy to see everything at Buxton Museum in a morning?	☐	☐
3 Was the mining village taken over by the people doing the reconstruction?	☐	☐
4 Were the buildings of interest in the area demolished?	☐	☐
5 Have the buildings been re-erected to display them to their best advantage?	☐	☐
6 Do the ponies get rid of the children?	☐	☐
7 Is the museum noticeably different from other museums in the country?	☐	☐
8 Can visitors inspect Buxton Open Air Museum every day of the week except Sundays?	☐	☐

EXERCISE THREE

Complete the following letter using words from the list below. There is one word for each gap and each word in the list can be used only once. Check your answers with the Key.

setting	turn	think	wear	take	turn	setting	throwing
~~taken~~	think	against	out	up	b~~a~~ck	out	about	of
		off	aside	~~away~~	with		

Dear Mr Wright,

I have to inform you that the staff and I are very much concerned over the behaviour of your son Thomas.

I am very sad to say that although Thomas is an intelligent and cheerful boy, he is one of the worst trouble-makers in the school. I believe that he has decided to _____ _____ authority and is _____ _____ to make his point by constantly challenging the system. However, he does not seem to realise that the system is there to help him and at the moment he is just _____ **away** his chances of a good education. Many members of staff have tried to _____ him _____ and to talk about his problems in a sensible way, but all this seems to have no effect. Thomas continues to disrupt classes and to challenge all the teachers' authority. I cannot _____ _____ any explanation. I cannot even say that he has **taken** _____ _____ a bad crowd as he is the one who leads the other children into mischief. Perhaps his need to cause trouble will _____ _____ over time, but meanwhile he is not only disturbing the whole school but he is _____ **back** his own academic achievement.

It is very important that we _____ _____ what is best for Thomas and best for the school. I should be grateful if you would arrange a suitable time to come into school, so that we can talk over this rather distressing problem. I am sure that everything will _____ _____ for the best.

Yours sincerely,

Alfred M. P. Hotchkiss (Headmaster)

EXERCISE FOUR

There are some words and letters missing from the sentences below. Use the missing words and letters to complete the puzzle.

1 He was such a good liar, she was taken __n. (1 letter)

2 The politician set _____ his party's standpoint. (5 letters)

3 The youngest child didn't take _____ anyone in the family. (5 letters)

4 He offered to stand in _____ the absent member of staff. (3 letters)

5 They say that after dark he turns ____to a wolf. (2 letters)

6 The teacher stood _____ the boy until he had finished his work. (4 letters)

7 She didn't know why, but she just didn't take ____ him. (2 letters)

8 The *nouveaux riches* can't resist showing _____ their wealth. (3 letters)

9 The gang of youths set ____ the boy they thought was the traitor. (2 letters)

EXERCISE FIVE

In a horoscope the writer makes predictions but cannot be 100% sure that the predictions will come true. In the following horoscopes, what words show that the writer is not 100% certain about the predictions? Read the horoscopes and check your answers with the Key. Then read the text again and answer the questions below.

Capricorn

Capricorns are usually cautious but you will need all your patience to keep close ones from doing something foolish. You may not be thanked for your help but your love and friendship will be valued in the long run. Take up a new sport to work off your frustrations.

Aquarius

If you feel that boredom has set in, this month will bring the change necessary to shake your life up and to get you moving again. From the 1st to the 6th you will experience an emotional period followed by renewed self-confidence. Social engagements with friends will bring you pleasure.

Pisces

Pisces is the sign of the gentle dreamer. But this month you could be surprised at what you can achieve if you stand up for your rights. Try to be more assertive and success will come your way. The end of the month may see you travelling abroad.

Aries
Arians are often so busy thinking about what they want next, they don't appreciate what they already have. You might benefit this month if you don't take on any new projects but think over what you have achieved and show your loved ones how you appreciate them. Making plans for a holiday could add to your relaxation.

Taurus
You will need to think over your relationships with other people this month. Taureans often pass over problems but this time you should try to face up to the facts and work on any relationships that matter to you. If the underlying tensions go, then things will only improve.

Gemini
The first few days of this month will be a good time to do all the jobs that you have put off for a long time. Finish all your outstanding work and be ready to face the future. Be prepared for romance and excitement between the 13th and 16th. You may meet a person who could turn your world upside down.

Cancer
Cancerians do not usually like change but this month may bring some surprises. You may meet some new people between the 11th and 16th: trust your first impressions, you can rely on them. The week of the 20th would be ideal to set aside some free time for a new hobby or pastime.

Leo
You will need to resist your natural tendency to show off and to be the extrovert. A quieter approach to life this month may bring unexpected friendship and harmony to your family life. On the 22nd you may feel a little depressed but the feeling will wear off by the 24th. Extra exercise or new clothes might cheer you up.

Virgo
You have a gift for organising and now your talents are in top gear. If others around you are making a mess of things, take charge. If things go a little wrong, apologise, you'll not be taken for a fool. Your sense of modesty will show you up in your best light. Virgo parents will need to be extra understanding and patient with their children on the 15th and 16th.

Libra
From the 6th to the 24th of this month you might find trouble in your close relationships. Don't work yourself up into a state, you will need all your Libran cool and balance. Avoid confrontation and the trouble will blow over. Don't try to take on everyone else's problems — give yourself a break and go away for a few days.

Scorpio

Take care this month as the planets are creating a major disturbance in your sign. You may set out with the best of intentions but things may not turn out as you planned. Stand back and take a good look at yourself. Is your forceful personality getting in the way of a more harmonious existence? After the 19th a calmer time is forecast.

Sagittarius

This month you will need to mix adventure and caution. You may hear of a good business deal or bargain on the 9th but beware, there may be unforeseen problems. On the 22nd the Sun moves back into your own sign, bringing back all your self-confidence. So don't throw up the chance to go on an adventure: it could turn your life around.

1 Which sign is advised to reserve some free time?

2 Which sign would be wrong to feel that boredom is permanent?

3 Which sign has very good intentions that may go bad?

4 Which sign will not be thought foolish if they apologise?

5 Which sign loves to boast?

6 Which sign is advised to defend their rights?

7 Which sign is advised not to accept any new work?

8 Which sign is advised to try a new sport?

9 Which sign should consider their personal relationships at length?

10 Which sign is promised a meeting with someone who could change their life?

11 Which sign is promised an adventure that could send their life in a different direction?

12 Which sign is advised to stay calm?

EXERCISE SIX

How would you feel if you were Auntie Susan and you received this letter from 'your loving niece Candy'?

Rose's Way
14th September

Dear Auntie Susan,

I was rather taken aback when I heard from Claud that you have decided to give all your money to a cats' home when you die.

Perhaps you hope we will think it is a ~~charitable~~ kind gesture, but I'm afraid that I can see through it. I believe that you intend to take away from your family what is rightfully theirs.

You must have been setting aside money over the years for your loved ones and I wonder why you now set out to upset us all.

You should think about your dear little grand nephew and grand niece and how they will suffer. They will not be able to have a private education, they will no longer have wonderful summer holidays in the Caribbean. Please don't turn them against you by ~~doing~~ making this thoughtless gesture.

Please think over what I have said. I hope that all of us and the solicitors can work something out.

Your loving niece,

Candy

Write a reply to this letter. Talk about each point that your niece makes. Write informally and remember that you are probably angry and possibly upset.